THE ART OF PHILOSOPHIZING
AND OTHER ESSAYS

THE ART OF PHILOSOPHIZING AND OTHER ESSAYS

by

BERTRAND RUSSELL

1977

LITTLEFIELD, ADAMS & CO.
Totowa, New Jersey

Published 1974 by

LITTLEFIELD, ADAMS & CO.

by arrangement with Philosophical Library, Inc.

Copyright, 1968, by Philosophical Library, Inc.

Reprinted 1977

Library of Congress Cataloging in Publication Data

Russell, Bertrand Russell, 3rd Earl, 1872–1970
   The Art of Philosophizing, and Other Essays

   (A Littlefield, Adams Quality Paperback No. 273)

   Reprint of the ed. published by the Philosophical Library,
New York.

   1.   Philosophy—Addresses, essays, lectures.

1.   Title.
[B1649.R91   1974]   192   74–1277
ISBN 0-8226-0273-3

Printed in the United States of America

CONTENTS

PUBLISHER'S PREFACE

The essays in this little volume, published here for the first time in book form, were written by Bertrand Russell during the second World War.

In those years the author was teaching philosophy at American universities, exercising a growing influence on America's student population.

The essays assembled here are fundamentally concerned with "the art of reckoning" in the fields of mathematics, logic and philosophy.

The simplicity of Russell's exposition is astonishing, as is his ability to get to the core of the great philosophical issues and to skillfully probe the depth of philosophical analysis.

The Art of Rational Conjecture

*L*ET us begin with a few words as to what philosophy is. It is not definite knowledge, for that is science. Nor is it groundless credulity, such as that of savages. It is something between these two extremes; perhaps it might be called "The art of rational conjecture." According to this definition, philosophy tells us how to proceed when we want to find out what may be true, or is *most likely* to be true, where it is impossible to know with certainty what *is* true. The art of rational conjecture is very useful in two different ways. First: often the most difficult step in the discovery of what *is* true is thinking of a hypothesis which *may* be true; when once the hypothesis has been thought of, it can be tested, but it may require a man of genius to think of it. Second: we often have to act in spite of uncertainty, because delay would be dangerous or fatal; in such a case, it is useful to possess an art by which we can judge what is probable. This art, so far as very general hypotheses are concerned, is philosophy. Particular questions, such as "will it rain tomorrow?" do not belong to philosophy; philosophy is concerned with general questions, such as: "Is the world governed by mechanical laws, or has it a cosmic purpose, or has it both characteristics at once?" Philosophy examines whether anything can be said on such general questions.

The first thing to realize, if you wish to become a philosopher, is that most people go through life with a whole world of beliefs that have no sort of rational justification, and that one man's world of beliefs is apt to be incompatible with another man's, so that they cannot both be right. People's opinions are mainly designed to make them feel comfortable; truth, for most people is a secondary consideration. You, dear readers, have of course no prejudices; but you will admit that in this you are different from most people. I shall suppose that you are a Baptist from Tennessee. It is obvious to you that America is the greatest country in the world, that Tennessee is the most distinguished of the States, and that the Baptists are the sole repositories of theological truth. Let us suppose that I concede all this. What am I to say to a man from another State or another country? How can I persuade a French Canadian Catholic of the truths which are so luminously evident to you? There are still a good many points about which you and he will agree, but how if you have to argue with a Turk or a Hindu or a Confucian? You will find them questioning most of what you have accepted as unquestionable, and if you are to argue profitably with them you will have to find common ground beneath your respective assumptions.

You will still find some things about which you can agree with the Turk. Are men descended from monkeys? Perish the thought! Is man the supreme glory of the universe? Of course. On such matters your common humanity makes you see eye to eye. But if one day an intelligent being were to arrive from Mars, he might turn out to be as superior to men as men are to monkeys; he might think the difference between men and monkeys very slight, and consider it obvious that they had a common ancestry. He would assert the claims of Mars (unless he were a philosopher) as confidently as you had asserted the claims of Tennessee. And what could you do about it?

If you wish to become a philosopher, you must try, as far as you can, to get rid of beliefs which depend solely upon the place and time of your education, and upon what your parents and schoolmasters told you. No one can do this completely, and no one can be a perfect philosopher, but up to a point we can all achieve it if we wish to. "But why should we wish to?" you may ask. There are several reasons. One of them is that irrational opinions have a great deal to do with war and other forms of violent strife. The only way in which a society can live for any length of time without violent strife is by establishing social justice, and social justice appears to each man to be injustice if he is persuaded that he is superior to his neighbors. Justice between classes is difficult where there is a class that believes itself to have a right to more than a proportionate share of power or wealth. Justice between nations is only possible through the power of neutrals, because each nation believes in its own superior excellence. Justice between creeds is even more difficult, since each creed is convinced that it has a monopoly of the truth of the most important of all subjects. It would be increasingly easier than it is to arrange disputes amicably and justly if the philosophic outlook were more wide-spread.

A second reason for wishing to be philosophic is that mistaken beliefs do not, as a rule, enable you to realize good purposes. In the middle ages, when there was an epidemic of plague, people crowded into the churches to pray, thinking that their piety would move God to take pity on them; in fact, the crowds in ill-ventilated buildings provided ideal conditions for the spread of the infection. If your means are to be adequate to your ends, you must have knowledge, not merely superstition or prejudice.

A third reason is that truth is better than falsehood. There is something ignominious in going about sustained by comfortable lies. The deceived husband is traditionally ludicrous, and there is something of the same laughable or pitiable quality about all happiness that depends upon being deceived or deluded.

If you wish to become a philosopher, you must train both the intellect and the emotions. The two sorts of training are intimately interconnected, but they must be to some extent separated in discussion. I shall begin with the training of the intellect.

The training of the intellect has both a positive and a negative aspect: you have to learn what to believe, and what not to believe. Let us begin with the positive aspect.

Although, in the last analysis, everything may be more or less doubtful, yet some things are so nearly certain that for all practical purposes the element of doubt may be ignored. The would-be philosopher will ask himself what kinds of knowledge seem least open to question, and why. He may, in starting this inquiry, reasonably assume that the most certain kinds of knowledge are those about which there is least dispute. He will soon find that these are not the kinds of knowledge, or supposed knowledge, that are asserted with most vehemence. Everyone is agreed about the multiplication table, but no one goes about proclaiming that it contains Sacred Truth. If anyone were to deny its truth, he would not be burnt at the stake or imprisoned as a fifth columnist. A sensible man, if he fell among arithmetical heretics, and were asked to recant his belief in the multiplication table, would do so, conscious that his recantation could do the multiplication table no harm. These are the characteristics of a belief about which there is no reasonable doubt.

Whoever wishes to become a philosopher will do well to acquire a considerable knowledge of mathematics. In the course of this study he will get to know what sorts of truths can be discovered by mere thinking, without the help of observation. He will also acquire familiarity with exact reasoning, and with the sort of mistakes to which even very expert reasoners are prone. For this last purpose, he will do well to study mathematics historically. For example: before Einstein, everybody thought it had been proved mathematically that gravitation is propagated instantaneously, but Einstein's theory required that it should be propagated with the velocity of light. Sure enough, the mathematicians found a mistake in the argument which had satisfied them for generations, and now, unless they are Nazis, they are all agreed that Einstein was right about the velocity of gravitation. This, however, was a very advanced and difficult question; it would be a mistake to be led by this instance into a general skepticism about mathematics. What it is right to infer is that, where questions are concerned that are both more complex and more nearly related to our passions than the questions of mathematics, the chance of errors in reasoning becomes very great. This applies especially to social and religious questions.

Logic is useful to the philosopher in its modern form, not in the musty medieval form that the schoolmen produced out of Aristotle. It is useful chiefly as teaching caution in inference. Those who are not trained in logic are prone to inferences that have no validity. For example, if one class or nation is oppressed by another, and you think this oppression ought to cease, they will expect you to regard the oppressed class or nation as possessed of superior virtue, and will be surprised if you do not feel a personal liking for each and every one of them. There is here no logical connection, although to an untrained mind there seems to be one. The more expert you become in logic, the fewer will be the inferences that you allow to be valid, and the seldomer will you regard it as inconsistent to hold two opinions at once. This is important practically, since it allows necessary compromise, and prevents acceptance of some rigid bloc of opinions. Blocs of opinions, such as Catholicism, Communism, or Nazism, tend to be persecuting, and are practically certain to be at least partly false. Practice in logical analysis makes it harder to be satisfied with such ready-made mental clothing.

Logic and mathematics, useful as they are, are only intellectual training for the philosopher. They help him to know how to study the world, but they give him no actual information about it. They are the alphabet of the book of nature, not the book itself.

The knowledge that is needed above all, if you wish to become a philosopher, is knowledge of science—not in its minute detail, but in its general results, its history, and especially its method. It is science that makes the difference between the modern world and the world before the 17th Century. It is science that has destroyed the belief in witchcraft, magic and sorcery. It is science that has made the old creeds and the old superstitions impossible for intelligent men to accept. It is science that has made it laughable to suppose the earth the center of the universe and man the supreme purpose of the creation. It is science that is showing the falsehood of the old dualisms of soul and body, mind and matter, which have their origin in religion. It is science that is beginning to make us understand ourselves, and to enable us, up to a point, to see ourselves from without as curious mechanisms. It is science that has taught us the way to substitute tentative truth for cocksure error. The scientific spirit, the scientific method, the framework of the scientific world, must be absorbed by any one who wishes to have a philosophic outlook belonging to our time, not a literary antiquarian philosophy fetched out of old books. Assuredly Plato was a man of great genius, and Aristotle was comprehensively encyclopedic; but in their modern disciples they can inspire only error. An hour with Galileo or Newton will give you more help towards a sound philosophy than a year with Plato and Aristotle. But if you go to a university, this will not be the opinion of your professors.

Science, we said, is important to the philosopher in its results and in its method. Let us say something about each of those in turn.

As regards results: the first thing of importance to the philosopher is the history of the universe, past and future. The earlier and later parts are conjectural, but there is a long stretch in the middle about which there is not much doubt. It seems that, a good while ago, there was a diffused nebula, something like a very thin mist; some parts were not quite so thin as others, and these gradually became stars. Our star, the sun, either because another star passed near it or for some different reason, gave birth to a number of planets, which, at first, were as hot as their parent, but being smaller they presently cooled. One of them, when it reached a suitable temperature, generated certain chemically complex structures having the property of being able to confer their own composition and structure on suitable neighboring matter. This property is called *life*. Living structures became gradually more complex as they evolved through the animal and vegetable kingdoms; one of the most complex is man. The existence of life depends upon a number of conditions, chemical and thermal. For countless ages the weather was too hot for life; perhaps in the end it will be too cold. But some astronomers, for instance Sir James Jeans, tell us that before it grows too cold the sun will burst, which will cause the earth and all the other planets to become gaseous. In one way or in another, it is pretty certain that life on earth will presently cease.

The universe is on a large scale, both in time and space. The sun is almost 93 million miles from the earth, and its light reaches us in eight minutes. The nearest of the stars are so distant that their light takes several years to reach us. All the stars we see with the naked eye are part of the milky way, which is one of a vast number of star-clusters. In addition to star-clusters there are nebulae—something like a million of them—which are incredibly remote, so remote that their light takes many hundreds of thousands of years to reach us, although it travels at the rate of 180,000 miles a second. As for the time-scale, the earth has existed for millions of years, but its beginning is recent as compared to the beginnings of the sun. When Sir James Jeans speaks of the possibility of the sun bursting, one gets at first an impression that this catastrophe is imminent, but in the end he consolingly suggests that it will not happen for a million years. The universe, we are told, is steadily tending towards a state in which energy will be uniformly distributed, and therefore useless for all the purposes which it serves at present. When that time comes, and probably long before it, life will be extinct everywhere, and only a miracle could restore it. Even the most religious men of science, unless they are Catholics, agree that these are the most probable conclusions on the present evidence.

Let us contrast this picture of the universe with that presented in the Bible and the Fathers, which was generally accepted throughout Christendom until science caused men to question it. According to the Bible and the Fathers, the universe was created in six days by God's fiat; the date of the creation can be computed from the data in Genesis, and has been estimated at B.C. 4004. The earth is the center of the universe, and the creation of Adam and Eve was the last act in God's work. God told them not to eat of the fruit of a certain tree, and when they nevertheless did so, He was very angry, although He had always known that they would disobey Him. He was so angry that He decided on an infinite punishment: they and all their progeny deserved to burn eternally in an everlasting fire. But God the Son took upon himself the punishment due to a certain portion of mankind, by suffering crucifixion and spending three days in hell. In virtue of His suffering, those who hold correct theological opinions and undergo certain ceremonies will go to heaven instead of hell. The visible world will pass away at Christ's second coming, the date of which is uncertain. The first disciples believed it to be imminent; then it was expected in 1000 A.D. Some Protestant sects still think that it will come within a few years. After that there will be only heaven and hell—and purgatory for a while, according to the Catholics.

Let us note some of the differences between these two conceptions of the universe. There is first the difference of scale: the Christian universe was small and of brief duration (apart from heaven and hell), while the scientific universe is not known to have a beginning or end in either time or space, and is certainly of unimaginable extent in both. In the Christian universe, everything had a purpose and everything had its place; it was neat and tidy, like a good housewife's kitchen. Another difference is that the

Christian universe centered about the earth, while the scientific universe has no center; in the Christian universe, the earth was fixed, and the celestial spheres revolved about it, while in the scientific universe *everything* is in motion. The Christian universe was made for man, while the scientific universe, if it is made to serve any end, is made to serve one which we cannot imagine. Indeed the whole conception of purpose, which dominated pseudo-scientific thought during the 2,000 years from Aristotle to the 17th Century, has disappeared from modern scientific explanations. Why the laws of nature are what they are is a question which science has ceased to ask, because there is no reason to suppose that it has an answer. Moral conceptions, such as sin and punishment, dominated the Christian scheme, which in the scientific scheme have no place. The Christian universe was such as uninstructed men might expect the universe to be, while the scientific universe blandly ignores our prejudices and our hopes, our loves and our hates.

Above all these differences, there is the difference of evidence. The evidence for the Christian scheme of things is the Bible; the evidence for the scientific world is observation and induction. Science asks on what ground the Bible account should be accepted. Were the authors of the Pentateuch present at the Creation? Obviously not. Can we believe that God revealed the truth to them? There are great difficulties in this view. The Bible is not the only Sacred Book; other religions have different cosmologies. How is an impartial inquirer to know which to believe? The Bible sometimes contradicts itself; it gives two quite inconsistent accounts of the creation of Adam and Eve, and in one place it says there were two sheep in the ark while in another it says there were seven. Then there are other difficulties. The Jesuit Acosta, who lived in South America, was puzzled by the animals only to be found there, though all must have come from Mount Ararat. This was especially puzzling in the case of the sloth, which is so dilatory in its motions that it could hardly have reached South America in the time since the flood. Sailors might, of course, have brought the various queer beasts from the old world, but the worthy Father thinks this unlikely, especially in the case of the filthy Acacias, of which the smell is unendurable.

Then there were troubles about fossils, which seemed to prove the world older than it could be if Genesis were true. Gradually belief in the literal truth of Genesis came to be very generally abandoned, and the way was left clear for acceptance of the scientific account.

What science has to say about very distant times and places is said with hesitation; it is set forth as what is most probable on the existing evidence, but any day new evidence may lead to new conclusions on this point or that. It is unlikely, however, that the general picture will be very much changed. What theology had to say, before science had weakened its authority, was said with a very different accent: what it pronounced was truth eternal, unalterable, unquestionable. Those who questioned it deserved to be burnt here on earth, as Giordano Bruno was burnt, and they would certainly burn hereafter to the end of time. No theologian would say this now, but that is because even infallible dogmas have had to be surreptitiously modified to meet the onslaught of science.

Whoever wishes to become a philosopher will do well to pay attention to the history of science, and particularly to its warfare with theology. With the exception of pure mathematics, every science has had to begin by fighting to establish its right to exist. Astronomy was condemned in the person of Galileo, geology in the person of Buffon. Scientific medicine was, for a long time, made almost impossible by the opposition of the Church to the dissection of dead bodies. Darwin came too late to suffer penalties, but Catholics and the Legislature of Tennessee still regard evolution with abhorrence. Each step has been won with difficulty, and each new step is still opposed, as if nothing were to be learnt from past defeats.

In our day, it is the newest science, psychology, that encounters opposition, particularly when it seems in danger of interfering with the doctrine of "sin." In any human community, some people act in ways inimical to the interests of the community; if social life is to continue, it is necessary to find ways of preventing such anti-social behavior. The conception of "sin" was the Church's way of effecting this object. If the police failed, the sinner could not congratulate himself on his escape, for God would punish him. This method had a certain efficacy in certain kinds of cases. But we now know that much anti-social behavior has deep psychological causes, and will not cease until those causes are removed by psychological curative treatment. Much of what used to be indiscriminately labelled "sin" turns out to be more of the nature of disease, amenable perhaps to medical treatment, but not to punishment. Those who take this attitude are accused by the orthodox of advocating whatever "sins" should, in their opinion, be treated medically rather than penally. This is simply the old opposition to science, taking courage from the fact that psychology, the science in question, is still young and immature. In ethics, equally, the old obscurantism continues. No one is injured when a man marries his deceased wife's sister, and yet the Church is still shocked by such wicked behavior, since it defines "sin" not as what does harm, but as what the Bible or the Church condemns.

It is time to say something about scientific method. Science is concerned to discover general laws, and is interested in particular facts chiefly as evidence for or against such laws. Geography and history are interested in particular facts on their own account, but neither is a science except in so far as it is able to discover general laws. It must be realized that we might live in a world without general laws, where bread would be nourishing one day and stones the next, where Niagara would sometimes fall up instead of down, and kettles would occasionally freeze when put on the stove. All this would be awkward, but it would not be logically impossible. Fortunately, our world is different. By the time we begin to think, we have become accustomed to a number of regularities — day and night, summer and winter, seed-time and harvest, and so on. With regard to things that seem irregular, like thunderstorms, two hypotheses were initially possible. It might be that there were regularities, though too complex to be easily discovered; or it might be that such phenomena were due to capricious deities. The latter view was universally adopted by primitive men, and survived among the clergymen of Boston until the time of Benjamin Franklin. These worthy men maintained that the lightning conductor was impious, and had led, through God's wrath, to an increase of earthquakes. The world, however, has decided against them.

Gradually it has come to be accepted that all natural phenomena are governed by general laws, though these laws, in the case of the minutest quantum transitions, are only statistical. The discovery of general laws is sometimes very difficult; it proved easiest in the study of the solar system. Kepler proved that Mars goes round the sun in an ellipse, and gave grounds, though not conclusive ones, for supposing that the other planets do likewise. Then Newton discovered the law of gravitation, which lasted without modification for over 200 years. Tiny discrepancies led Einstein to a change which was in practice very minute, though very revolutionary as regards theory. Newton's law, it is now admitted, was not exactly right, although the errors in its predictions could only be discovered in a few cases, and then only by the utmost precision in measurement. This development may serve as a sample and model of scientific method. Hypothesis and observation alternate; each new hypothesis calls for new observations, and, if it is to be accepted, must fit the facts better than any previous hypothesis. But it always remains possible, if not probable, that some further hypothesis may be called for to explain further observations. New hypotheses do not show old ones to have been false, but only to have been approximations which were not quite exact, which is all that a wise man of science would ever claim for them.

The philosopher in search of knowledge, when he finds a scientific law generally accepted, may take it as probable that the law is approximately correct. To assume more than this would be rash.

So far, I have been considering the positive side of a philosopher's preliminary training; now it is time to consider the negative side. When I was a boy of about fifteen, I decided to look into all my beliefs, and discard them if they seemed to have no foundation except tradition or my own prejudices. Being a good deal of a prig, I intended to face one painful possibility every day; I began with the possibility that it might have been better if the English had lost the battle of Waterloo. After pondering this hypothesis for a long time, I found out one argument on Napoleon's side: that if he had won, England would have had the decimal system. I soon passed on to more important matters, such as the dogmas of the Christian religion, which I tried to examine impartially in spite of my strong desire to retain my faith. I think some such process is very useful to those who wish to become philosophers. It is easier to carry out effectively if you do not have to invent the arguments against your prejudices yourself, but have them presented to you by a person who believes them. It would be an admirable thing if all our schools contained a percentage of Moslems and Buddhists, who should be encouraged to defend their respective religions against the Christian majority among the pupils. This might diminish the strength of irrational conviction on both sides.

Another important element in negative training is the history of men's irrational beliefs. Aristotle asserted that women have fewer teeth than men, although he was a married man. Until the beginning of modern times, everybody thought that there is an animal, called the salamander, which lives in fire. Shakespeare repeats the superstition that the toad has a jewel in his head. These were not questions that roused people's passions; how much more, then, was error to be expected in matters as to which men had a strong bias? In the 16th Century, everybody believed in witchcraft—probably even the poor creatures who were condemned for it. History abounds in well-attested miracles which no modern man would accept. I do not allude, of course, to the miracles performed by Catholic Saints, but to those others, equally vouched for, that were performed by Arian or Nestorian or Monophysite heretics, or even by downright infidels. Nothing marvelous can be accepted on historical evidence, unless the evidence is of quite unusual strength. Men at all times have been prone to believe what subsequent ages proved to be false, and our time is no exception.

The training of the emotions is as important, in the making of a philosopher, as training of the intellect. It is important to be able to view human beings as products of circumstances. Given that certain sorts of people are more desirable than certain other sorts, it is a scientific question to discover how the more desirable sorts are to be made more common. The orthodox view is that this is to be done by preaching, but experience hardly supports this theory. All sorts of causes may lead a man to behave badly: faulty education, wrong diet, economic worries, and so on. It is a waste of energy to be angry with a man who behaves badly, just as it is to be angry with a car that won't go. The difference is that you can compel your car to go to a garage, but you cannot compel Hitler to go to a psychiatrist. You can, however, do something about the young potential Hitlers who exist everywhere, and who are also potential decent citizens. You will not do anything wise about these young people if you view them as "sinners."

It is important to learn not to be angry with opinions different from your own, but to set to work understanding how they come about. If, after you have understood them, they still seem false, you can then combat them much more effectually than if you had continued to be merely horrified.

I am not suggesting that the philosopher should have no feelings; the man who has no feelings, if there be such a man, does nothing, and therefore achieves nothing. No man can hope to become a good philosopher unless he has certain feelings which are not very common. He must have an intense desire to understand the world, as far as that is possible; and for the sake of understanding, he must be willing to overcome those narrownesses of outlook that make a correct perception impossible. He must learn to think and feel, not as a member of this or that group, but as just a human being. If he could, he would divest himself of the limitations to which he is subject as a human being. If he could perceive the world as a Martian or an inhabitant of Sirius, if he could see it as it seems to a creature that lives for a day and also as it would seem to one that lived for a million years, he would be a better philosopher. But this he cannot do; he is tied to a human body with human organs of perception. To what extent can this human subjectivity be overcome? Can we know anything at all about what the world *is*, as opposed to what it *seems?* This is what the philosopher wishes to know, and it is to this end that he has to undergo such a long training of impartiality.

Hitherto I have been concerned with the pre-philosophic training of the philosopher; it is only now that I come to the questions that are properly philosophical. When you have finished your training in logic and science, what should you do to apply your training to the problems that made you wish to become a philosopher?

If you ask an old-fashioned professor, he will tell you to read Plato and Aristotle, Kant and Hegel; also, as lesser luminaries, Descartes, Spinoza, and Leibniz; also, as awful warnings, Locke, Berkeley, and Hume. If you follow his advice, you will be able to pass examinations in what universities call "philosophy." You will have acquired, with considerable trouble, a lot of knowledge as to what these great men thought on various subjects. But unless you let your intelligence go to sleep while you are reading the "great" philosophers, you will not think that you have discovered what you yourself are to think on philosophical questions. It will be plain to you that a great deal of what these great men said is rubbish, and belonged to a pre-scientific mental atmosphere. Part of what they say is fallacious, part is clever guess-work. Clearly, if you want your problems solved, you must do the work yourself.

A man may be led to philosophy by any one of a number of problems. Let us take the problem we mentioned a moment ago:

Can we know anything about what the world is, as opposed to what it seems?

Let us first see how this problem arises. We see things with our eyes, and we imagine, until we reflect, that that is how things are. But animals see differently; they cannot appreciate pictures, though perhaps, if we knew how, we could make pictures that they would appreciate, though we should not. Flies have very curious eyes, which must make the world look very different to them from what it does to us. Whatever we see or hear—to take another point—seems to us to be happening now, but we know that light and sound take time to travel. The thunder, as a physical phenomenon, happens at the same time as the lightning, although we hear it later. When you see the sun setting, it "really" set eight minutes ago. When a new star appears, as sometimes happens, the event that you are seeing now may have happened thousands of years ago. Again: Physicists are agreed that color, as we experience it, is only in our perceptions; what corresponds, in the outer world, to color in our perceptions, are transverse waves, which are something quite different. The world of the physicist has only certain points in common with the world of the senses. The world of the senses, if supposed to exist outside us, is largely an illusion.

What would you say if you wished to meet this difficulty with the smallest possible departure from common sense? You would observe, as the physicist does, that, after all, we all live in a common world. Flies may have queer senses, but they gather round the honey-pot. In some sense, a number of people and animals can perceive the same event, though they perceive it differently. The differences must be subjective; what is common to all the perceivings may belong to the event itself, independently of our perceptive apparatus. This is, roughly, what the physicist supposes, and it seems a reasonable hypothesis. It cannot be regarded as certain, since there are other hypotheses that would account for all the known facts. But it has the merit that it cannot be disproved, and that it cannot lead to demonstrably false consequences, while it approaches as near to our naive beliefs as any hypothesis which is not refutable can do.

If you wish to deal with the problem completely, you will not stop at this point. You will try to find a method of formulating all the hypotheses that are compatible with all ascertainable facts. These must all agree in all their *verifiable* consequences, and therefore, for practical purposes, it makes no difference whatever which of them you adopt. If you can get as far as this, you have done all that is possible, since, though you have not arrived at one theory that *must* be true, you have shown that this is impossible, and have set out all the theories that *may* be true. More cannot be asked of a philosopher.

Let us take another philosophical problem: the relation of soul and body, or, more generally, of mind and matter. Common sense has come to take this dualism as a matter of course; we all regard it as obvious that we have a body and we have a mind. Philosophers, however, usually dislike dualism; some seek to avoid it by saying that the body is a phantom generated by the mind—these are called "idealists"—while others say that the mind is nothing but a way of behavior of the body—these are called "materialists." The distinction between mind and body did not always exist, but was made primarily in the interests of religion. It begins in Plato, who argued that the soul is immortal though the body is not. It was taken up and developed, in the last days of antiquity, first by the neo-platonists and then by the Christians. It is fully developed in the writings of St. Augustine. It is remarkable that a theory having such a purely philosophic and theological origin should have penetrated so deeply into the thought of ordinary men and women as to have come to seem almost self-evident. I think, however, that our would-be philosopher may profitably examine the whole distinction afresh, and that, if he does, he will come to think it much less obvious than it is generally supposed to be.

At first sight it may seem clear that when I think, that is an event in my mind, but when my arm moves, that is an event in my body. But what do I mean by "thinking"? And what do I mean by "my arm moving"? Neither is clear.

First as to "thinking." I experience pleasure and pain, I see and hear and touch things, I remember, I feel desire, and I make decisions; all these would be classified as "mental" events, and, in a large sense, might be called "thinking." Certainly such events occur, and therefore we are justified in saying that there is thinking. We are not justified, however, in saying further, as Descartes does, that there is a *thing* which thinks, and that this thing is my mind. To suppose that thoughts need a thinker is to be misled by grammar (or rather syntax). The thoughts can be perceived, but the thinker cannot; he is a piece of unnecessary metaphysical lumber.

And how about the motion of my arm? We all imagine, until we look into the question, that we know what "motion" is, and that we can see our arm moving. But this is a mistake. Motion is a physical phenomenon, and we must go to physics to find out what it is. Physics tells us an incredibly complicated story, according to which, though there is change, there is no such thing as motion, since this implies a "thing" which travels, and in quantum physics "things" have disappeared. We have, in place of them, strings of events related to each other in certain ways; such a string of events is what is mistakenly thought of as a "thing." About an arm as it appears in physics we know only certain abstract mathematical laws; we know so little that we cannot tell whether the events of which it is composed are like thoughts or unlike them. Thus all we can say is this: there are not two "things," my mind and my body; there is a series of events, called "thoughts," which are such that the later can remember the earlier; there is also, if physics is not mistaken, a series of events which is what is commonly thought of as my arm; but whether the events in the physical series are like thoughts or unlike them, it is impossible to know.

I do not mean that I am sure what I have just said is right; I say only that it seems to me probable. In any case, it is clear that the question of "mind" and "matter" cannot be fruitfully discussed in traditional terms, but only in terms which make it quite a different problem. To argue whether the soul is immortal, while having no idea what we mean by "soul," would obviously be futile. In this way, rather arid questions turn out to be necessary preliminaries to the discussion of matters of great emotional interest.

But perhaps you may say: I wished to become a philosopher because I thought philosophers knew the purpose of life, and could teach me how I ought to live; and hitherto you have not helped me in this way. Has philosophy nothing to say about such things?

This question deserves an answer, but the

answer cannot be quite simple. Philosophy, historically, is intermediate between science and religion; to the Greeks, it was a "way of life," but it was a way very largely concerned with the pursuit of knowledge. Some philosophers have emphasized the religious aspects of philosophy, others the scientific aspects; but always both have been present in a greater or lesser degree. A complete philosopher will have a conception of the ends to which life should be devoted, and will be in this sense religious; but he will be scientific because he thinks the pursuit of knowledge an essential part of the best life, and because he thinks knowledge necessary for the attainment of most of the things that he values. His moral and his intellectual life are thus closely intertwined.

The philosopher must think in general terms, because the problems with which he is concerned are general; and he must think impartially, because he knows that that is the only way to reach truth. Generality and impartiality in thought have their counterparts in purposes: his fundamental purposes, if he is a genuine philosopher, will be large and concerned with humanity as a whole. He will not be parochial, either in space or in time; people of other regions and other ages will be present to his imagination. Justice, in practical affairs, is closely allied to generality in intellectual matters. If you acquire the habit of thinking about the human race, you will find it increasingly difficult to confine your benevolence to a section of it. The stoics carried this principle so far as to condemn all particular affections, but in this they were mistaken. If you love no one in particular, your love of mankind will be cold and abstract. It is through private affection that love of mankind becomes warm and living. If, when you read of cruelties, you imagine them practiced on your wife or your child or your friend, you will feel a horror of them which would be impossible to a man who loved all human beings equally. The philosopher should not feel less than other men do for his friends or his country, but he should learn, in imagination, to generalize these feelings, and to allow to the friends and the countries of others the value which he assigns to his own.

The contemplation of immense distances and vast stretches of time, to which the philosopher should accustom himself, is capable of having a certain purifying effect upon the emotions. Some of the things about which we are inclined to grow excited seem puny and unimportant when brought into relation to the stellar universe; others, though they may seem less important than we had thought, do not seem unworthy. The doings of man have not that cosmic significance that could be attributed to them in the days of the Ptolemaic astronomy, but they are still all that we know of good and evil. To pursue personal greatness, like Ozymandias king of kings, is a trifle ridiculous, for the greatest power or fame attainable by a human being is still so microscopic as to be scarcely worth even a little effort. But impersonal aims—to try to understand as much of the world as possible, to create beauty, or to add to human happiness—do not seem laughable, since they are the best that we can do. And from the very knowledge of our unimportance it is possible to derive a certain kind of peace, which may make it less difficult to bear good fortune without vain glory and evil fortune without despair.

The Art of Drawing Inferences

*L*OGIC may be defined as the art of drawing inferences. Everybody draws inferences; in an important sense, even animals do so. But most people's ineferences are rash and hasty; subsequent experience shows them to be wrong. Logic aims at avoiding such unreliable kinds of inference; it is analogous to the rules of evidence in law. Often the inference is incapable of giving certainty, but can give a degree of probability sufficiently high for a reasonable man to act on it. The rules of *probable* inference are the most difficult part of logic, but also the most useful.

Logic was practically invented by Aristotle. For nearly two thousand years, his authority in logic was unquestioned. To this day, teachers in Catholic educational institutions are not allowed to admit that his logic has defects, and any non-Catholic who criticizes it incurs the bitter hostility of the Roman Church. I once ventured to do so on the radio, and the organizers who had invited me were inundated with protests against the broadcasting of such heretical doctrine. Undue respect for Aristotle, however, is not confined to Catholic institutions. In most universities, the beginner in logic is still taught the doctrine of the syllogism, which is useless and complicated, and an obstacle to a sound understanding of logic. If you wish to become a logician, there is one piece of advice which I cannot urge too strongly, and that is: Do NOT learn the traditional formal logic. In Aristotle's day it was a creditable effort, but so was the Ptolemaic astronomy. To teach either in the present day is a ridiculous piece of antiquarianism.

There are two sorts of logic, *deductive* and *inductive*. A deductive inference, if it is logically correct, gives as much certainty to the conclusion as the premises, while an inductive inference, even when it obeys all the rules of logic, only makes the conclusion probable even when the premises are deemed certain.

Deductive logic is useful when general premises are known, and also when they are assumed to see whether their consequences agree with experience. The great example of deductive logic is pure mathematics. In pure mathematics we start with general principles, and proceed to draw inferences from them. Whenever you do your accounts, you use deduction; the rules of arithmetic are assumed to be unquestionable, and you apply them to the particular figures representing your expenditure. Pure mathematics is a vast body of knowledge; even the greatest mathematicians know only a small fragment of it. Much of it is of the greatest practical utility, in navigation, in engineering, in war, and in many branches of modern industry. But when it is used in practical ways, it always has to be combined with other premises which have been obtained by induction. So long as it remains pure, it is a game, like solving chess problems; it differs from such games by the fact that it has applications.

Mathematics is not the only example of deductive logic, though it is the most important. Another example is law. I do not mean legislation, where the question is what law ought to be. I mean the business of the law-courts, which is concerned with what the law *is*. The laws, as enacted, lay down general principles, and the courts have to apply them to particular circumstances. Sometimes the logic is simple: murderers are to suffer the death penalty, this man is a murderer, therefore this man is to suffer the death penalty. But in more complicated cases, such as elaborate financial fraud, it may be very difficult to draw the necessary deductive inferences from the existing laws; if the swindler is sufficiently ingenious, there may be no laws applicable to his case.

Another deductive study is theology. From a logical point of view, this is closely similar to law; what the statutes are to the lawyer, the scriptures are to the theologian. Sometimes it is astonishing what pure deduction can achieve. St. Augustine deduced from St. Paul's epistle to the Romans that unbaptized infants go to hell, and that it is not virtue that gets people to heaven. The argument is able, and I think the conclusions are implicit in what St. Paul says, though I doubt whether the Apostle was aware of the implications. Perhaps if he had been he would have guarded himself against them.

The arguments of lawyers and theologians, though essentially deductive, are seldom in strict logical form, and usually introduce some empirical considerations over and above their general premises. Every pure deductive argument, when generalized to the utmost, will be found to belong to pure mathematics. In fact, pure mathematics and deductive logic are indistinguishable.

I do not mean that every deductive *argument* belongs to pure mathematics. This would not be true, because the material to which the argument applies may lie outside pure mathematics. Take the time-honored syllogism: "All men are mortal; Socrates is a man; therefore Socrates is mortal." Here "Socrates," "man," and "mortal" are known through our terrestrial experience; they have not the universality required of logic and mathematics. The corresponding pure logical principle is: "whatever A and B and C may be, if all A is B, and C is an A, then C is a B." Similarly "2 apples and 2 apples are 4 apples" is not a proposition of arithmetic, since it requires acquaintance with apples. It is deduced from the proposition of arithmetic that 2 and 2 are 4. It is only such entirely general statements that belong to logic or mathematics; and when we confine ourselves to such general statements, we shall find that there is no difference between mathematics and deductive logic. They are one subject, of which deductive logic, as ordinarily understood, is the earlier part, and pure mathematics, as ordinarily understood, the later part.

What can you learn by means of deduction? Perhaps, if you were sufficiently clever, you could learn nothing. Let us take an example from arithmetic. As soon as you know the multiplication table, you have the means of multiplying any two numbers, say 24657 and 35746. You apply the rules, and work it out. But if you were a calculating boy, you would "see" the answers, just as you "see" that 2 and 2 are 4. In fact, however, even calculating boys can't "see" the answer when the sum becomes difficult beyond a point. In practice, whenever the argument is at all complicated, we can only reach the conclusion by means of a process of deduction. It remains true that everything offered by deduction is, in a sense, already contained in the premises, but we only find out what is contained in the premises by means of the process of calculation.

The utility of deductive logic is great, but strictly limited. It will not tell you what to believe, but only that, *if* you believe A, you must believe B. *If* you believe the law of gravitation, you must believe what astronomers tell you about the movements of the planets. *If* you believe that all human beings are equal, you must be against slavery and in favor of votes for women. (It took people about a century to make this particular deduction.) *If* you believe that the whole of the Bible is true, you must believe that the hare chews the cud. Deduction tells you what follows from your premises, but does not tell you whether your premises are true.

It can, however, enable you to know that your premises are *false*. It may happen that the consequences of your premises can be disproved, and in that case your premises must be more or less wrong. Bishop Colenso, in his endeavor to convert the Zulus, translated the Bible into their language. They read it with an open mind, but when they came to the statement that the hare chews the cud they informed him that this was not the case. He was a bookish man, unfamiliar with the habits of hares, but at the instigation of the Zulus he observed a hare and found they were right. This caused him to have "doubts," which led the authorities to deprive him of his salary.

When a scientific theory is suggested, consequences open to observation are deduced from it, and if any of them turn out to be wrong the theory has to be discarded. Sometimes a theory may turn out to be self-contradictory, in the sense that, assuming the premises true, a deductive argument will show that they are false; this is *reductio ad absurdum*. In these ways, deduction is often a useful element in disproof.

Deduction plays a more positive part as an element in induction, where it helps to prove theories probably true. But of this I shall say more later.

Aristotle and the schoolmen thought of deductive logic as syllogistic. A syllogism is an argument with two premises, of which at least one must be general, and a conclusion drawn from them. It has to do with the relations of classes: given two classes A and

B, A may be part of B, A may lie wholly outside B, A may overlap with B, or part of A may lie outside B. The syllogism deduces a relation between A and C from relations of A and B and of B and C. For instance: If A lies inside B, and B lies outside C, then A lies outside C. If some of A is inside B, and all B is inside C, then some of A is inside C. And so on. A great many deductive arguments are not of this sort; in fact mathematics, which is deductive, seldom contains syllogisms. But the traditional logicians never noticed this. Nor did they notice that there are simpler kinds of deduction than the syllogism—except in the case of what are called "immediate inferences," such as "If John is the father of James, then James is the son of John." The modern theory of deduction only arrives at the relations of classes after going through a good deal that is logically simpler. It should be noted that what is logically simplest is by no means the same thing as what strikes a beginner as easiest.

I come now to inductive logic, which is more useful than the deductive kind, but raises much greater difficulties. In fact, the philosophy of induction contains unsolved problems, which have been something of a scandal ever since the time of Hume. Nevertheless, if you wish to practice inductive logic in a proficient manner, there is a definite technique to be learnt. No one doubts that the technique works; the difficulties are as to *why* it works.

Induction starts, psychologically, from an animal propensity. An animal which has had experience of things happening in a certain way will behave as if it expected them to happen the same way next time. If you drive your horse by a certain road very often, he will automatically take that road if you let him alone, and it may even be quite difficult to make him take a different road. In this a horse differs from a motor car, which never gets to know what road you usually take. Domestic animals get to know their feeding time, and expect food from the person who usually feeds them. This sort of thing, of course, is not a formulated belief in the animal, but merely a habit of behavior. However, if the animal could be taught to talk, it would verbalize its habits, and say "of course so-and-so will feed me; he always does." The unsophisticated savage can and does say this sort of thing, and so do children.

A great many of our every-day beliefs, though science may be able to give some learned ground for them, are in fact merely based upon this law of animal habit. We expect the sun to rise tomorrow, because it always has risen. When we are about to eat an apple, we expect it to taste like an apple and not like a beefsteak, because that is the way apples always have tasted. If you see half of a horse which is coming toward you round the corner, you expect the other half to be horse and not cow, because you have never seen an animal of which the front half looked like a horse and the back half like a cow. These expectations are not intellectual; you do not first examine your data and then reach a conclusion. If you are falling and expect a bump, you do not go through an argument about the impact of falling bodies with hard ground; your expectation, though it may be *caused* by previous bumps, is not, in any logical sense, *inferred* from them. Experience seems capable of being stored up in the body, and of giving rise to expectations which are physiological rather than mental. In the case mentioned above, where you see half a horse, you probably do not have any *conscious* expectation as to the other half, but if the other half turned out to be cow, you would experience a violent shock of surprise, showing that expectation had been present, even if below the conscious level.

Inductive logic is an attempt to justify this animal propensity, in so far as it can be justified. It cannot be justified completely, for after all, surprising things do sometimes happen. A chicken may have been fed by a certain man throughout its life, and have come to look to him confidently for food; but one day he wrings its neck instead. It would have been better for the chicken if its inductive inferences had been less crude. Inductive logic aims at telling you what kinds of inductive inferences are least likely to lead you to suffer the tragic disillusionment of the chicken. It appears that, even at the best, you can never be *certain* that an inductive inference will prove sound, but there are ways by which you can indefinitely diminish the probability of error, until you reach a point where every sensible man will regard the conclusion as sufficiently established for purposes of action. It might be said that the whole theory of induction is negative. The savage makes utterly reckless inductions; civilized people who have not learnt scientific method are still apt to be rash; but the man who has learnt inductive logic allows himself only a few of the inductions towards which he feels an animal propensity. Why he should permit these few, is an obscure question; but his reasons for abstaining from the others are fairly definite.

The most elementary form of induction is "simple enumeration." this says: In all the cases known to me, A has always been followed (or accompanied) by B; therefore probably the next A that I come across will be followed (or accompanied) by B, and, somewhat less probably, A will always be followed (or accompanied) by B. Our bodies, and the bodies of animals, are so made that, unless we exert deliberate restraint, we shall act as if we believed in the validity of induction by simple enumeration, but, as we have seen, such action will sometimes lead us astray. Night has always been followed by day, therefore we naturally expect that it always will be; but some astronomers say that, in time, tidal friction will cause the earth always to turn the same face to the sun, and then night will no longer be followed by day. There was once a Stoic philosopher who was invited to dine with Ptolemy, king of Egypt. The king, for a joke, gave him a pomegranate made of wax, which the philosopher incautiously bit into. He was allowing himself the general inductive belief: "what looks like a pomegranate tastes like one." If you give a savage a box containing a gyrostat, he will think it bewitched, because he cannot turn it. Witchcraft and sorcery are convenient notions for explaining away inductions that go wrong.

We cannot ultimately escape from induction by simple enumeration, but we can immensely strengthen it by means of general laws. In this way, everything becomes an instance of a much wider generalization than that which originally gave rise to our inductive belief. The wider generalization may enable us to know when the original one will fail, and may show the presence of regularity where at first sight there seemed to be none. Take, for instance, the belief that the sun will rise tomorrow. In primitive man, this belief has no logical grounds, but it has causes; the causes are his own experiences of day following night, and the testimony of his elders that this has always happened so far as memory and tradition extend. Reflection turns these causes into grounds, but science provides new grounds that are much stronger. The sun rises because the earth rotates; the laws governing rotation are the laws of dynamics; and the laws of dynamics are confirmed by all observations of relevant phenomena, whether on earth or in the heavens. Thus these laws, because of their great generality, are confirmed by many more instances than there are of the sun rising. But these laws themselves are still accepted on a basis of simple enumeration. The only essential gain is that the instances enumerated are much more numerous than in the subordinate generalizations from which we started.

The process that we have been considering depends upon the discovery of general laws, and general laws cannot be discovered unless they exist. One could imagine a universe without general laws, or at any rate without any sufficiently simple for us to discover them. Obviously we could not remain alive in such a universe. Animals use the general law "what smells good is good." This has exceptions, which enable us to poison rats and ants. But unless the exceptions were exceptional, animals could not decide what to eat, or, if they did decide, they would be poisoned as often as not. We, by the help of the microscope, have arrived at better general laws, and have learnt to reject milk that smells good but is tubercular. But if there were no general laws, it might happen tomorrow that any milk which is *not* tubercular would make us ill. If there were no general laws, there would be no possible way of knowing what to do.

It is true that, for practical purposes, we could make shift to do with general laws that are *usually* true; our food would *sometimes* poison us, but so it does at present. In fact, science professes to have found general laws that are *always* true, and there is no reason to doubt that there are such laws, whether or not they are exactly those in which science at present believes. Scientific method is essentially a method of discovering laws. Assuming that there are general laws, let us consider how to set about discovering them.

Our principle of simple enumeration considered the case where some kind of occurrence A is always followed or accompanied by an occurrence of another kind B. This, by itself, is not always a very good ground for an induction. Uneducated people in China believe that an eclipse of the moon is caused by an attempt of the Heavenly Dog to eat the moon. Therefore when an eclipse occurs they come out and beat gongs loudly, to frighten away this dangerous celestial animal. I once saw an eclipse of the moon at Changsha, and heard the deafening din of the gongs. Sure enough, the eclipse presently stopped; and this has been the experience in China from time immemorial. Why, then, should we not believe that the gongs help to dispel the eclipse? We have, of course, the evidence of eclipses not visible in China, but that is mere luck; if the Chinese superstition were universal, this evidence would not exist.

The evidence for a general law is better when A and B are both measurable quantities, and it is found that the more there is of A the more there is of B. The hotter the fire, the sooner the kettle boils. This is called the principle of "concomitant variations." Many people who profess to be weather-wise think that the weather changes with the phases of the moon, but careful observation shows that this is not the case. On the other hand, the tides do change with the moon: spring tides occur just after new moon and full moon, neap tides just after first and third quarters. Therefore there clearly is a law connecting the moon with the tides.

Or, again, take the law that bodies expand as the temperature rises. What does this law really say? We think of temperature, unscientifically, as what makes us feel hot or cold, but this is only roughly true. A calm day with the thermometer at 70° will feel hotter than a windy day with the thermometer at 80°. So we define temperature by the thermometer, not by our feelings. We then find that all bodies, except water which is near the freezing point, take up more room at a high temperature than at a low one. When many experiments have confirmed this, we cannot regard it as an accidental coincidence, and we allow ourselves to be-

lieve that there is a general law to this effect.

The instance that made the greatest impression upon the scientific world was the
law of gravitation. Newton discovered that
every planet at every instant has an acceleration towards the sun, which, for all of them,
varies as the square of the distance from
the sun. A law of this sort collects together,
not only actual past data, but an infinite
number of future possible data. If these all
work out as the law has led us to expect, we
soon become convinced that the law must
be right, at least within the errors of observation.

Induction is connected with probability,
not only in the sense that the conclusion of
an inductive inference is never more than
probable, but also in other ways. For instance: if a hypothesis which fits all the
known facts leads you to predict something
that seems very improbable, and then your
prediction comes true, it makes it seem highly probable that your hypothesis was right.
Suppose I wish to acquire credit as a weather prophet. If, in July, I say "tomorrow there
will be a thunderstorm," and then there is

one, my friends may say it was only a lucky guess. But if, in January, I say "tomorrow there will be a thunderstorm with a heavy fall of snow," and then there is one, they will be more impressed. If I say "tomorrow Hitler will make a bombastic speech," and my prophecy comes true, no one will be much surprised. But if I say "tomorrow Hitler will give up his position as Fuhrer and become a monk," and then it happens, everybody will be struck with my capacities as a prophet, or think that I am more in the confidence of the Nazis than I ought to be. The more improbable your prophecy, the more your hypothesis is confirmed when what you predict happens.

Now in all the advanced sciences the laws are quantitative, and enable exact predictions to be made—as exact, that is to say, as our measuring instruments render it possible to confirm. Now apart from some scientific law, any quantitatively exact prophecy would be infinitely unlikely to be true. Let us take an illustration. Suppose I say "the next man we meet will weigh between 130 and 170 pounds," you will say "very likely; most men do." And if I turn out to have been right you will say "well, you didn't risk much." If I say he will weigh between 149 and 151 pounds, and he does, it will be a little more remarkable. But suppose I say "he will weigh 150.0001 pounds," and we find, using the best balance we can find in a physical laboratory, that this is his weight as nearly as it can be ascertained, you will ask me how I could have known. Now scientific predictions are generally of this kind. They foretell the exact time when an eclipse of the sun will begin and end, the exact position of Jupiter at a given moment, and so on. If one could take the word "exact" strictly, this would be so remarkable as to be almost incredible; even allowing for the margin of error in observations, it is astonishing.

The discovery of Neptune was a feat of this sort, which gave the general public a great respect for the astronomers. The planet Uranus did not behave quite as it ought; two men, Adams and Leverrier, attributed this behavior to an unknown planet, the position of which they calculated. When it was looked for, it was found in the place where they said it would be. What made this event impressive was that, apart from their calculations, it would have been so very improbable that a planet would be found at any given place.

But prediction, however spectacular, is by no means conclusive. It often happens that two quite different hypotheses have the same consequences over a wide field, and in that case, when the consequences are verified, this does not enable us to choose between the two hypotheses. Einstein's law of gravitation is, philosophically and logically, very different from Newton's, but its observable consequences are nearly identical. In such a case, it is necessary to look out for something as to which the observable consequences of the two hypotheses would be different; if the consequences are found to suit one hypothesis and not the other, the one provisionally holds the field. This was what happened in the famous eclipse observations in 1919. Newtonians were prepared to admit that the light rays from the stars that were nearly in line with the sun might be deflected a certain calculated amount by the sun's gravitation, but Einstein said they would be deflected twice as much as this. He turned out to be right, and so his emendation of Newton's law was accepted. But the evidence for Einstein's law is only slightly better than the evidence for Newton's used to be, and at any moment some further modification may prove necessary. This is characteristic of science: dogmatic certainty is neither sought nor achieved.

One of the most important and difficult things about inductive method is the discovery of fruitful analogies, and the connected problem of the analysis of a complex phenomenon into elements that can be studied separately. The fruitful analogy is one that discloses a similarity in causation, and the investigator has to begin by guessing at the cause. If earthquakes are due to the wrath of God, the analogous phenomena are plagues, pestilences, famines, and comets. So the middle ages believed. But to a modern investigator quite different analogies suggest themselves. I remember reading of a physicist who was for a time in Tokio, and accordingly took an interest in earthquakes. After he had developed a mathematical theory concerned with them, he applied it to the vibrations of the plates of locomotives, which had been annoying railroad companies. To us, to take another illustration, the analogy between lightning and the electric spark is obvious; but to the middle ages it would seem that the cause of a man's being struck by lightning was likely to be his sinful life. Modern men, studying thunderstorms, asked themselves: "What state of the atmosphere is present during thunderstorms and absent at other times?" When a man has made a guess at the answer to such a question, he tries to produce analogous conditions on a small scale in his laboratory, or, if that is impossible, to look for other natural phenomena which resemble the one he is studying in what he thinks may be the essential characteristic. Only the result can show whether his guess was right.

The purpose of inductive logic is to infer general laws from particular occurrences. Deductive logic does the opposite; it *starts* with general premises, and is therefore faced with the question: How do we come to know these premises? In pure mathematics, the answer is that we know them because they are purely verbal. The statement "two and two are four" is like the statement "there are three feet to a yard." We don't have to verify this by observation, because it is not a law of nature, but a decision of our own as to how we are going to use words. That is why pure mathematics is able to get on without observation or experiment.

But outside logic and pure mathematics the question of general premises cannot be so easily solved. Take once more the stock syllogism of traditional formal logic: "All men are mortal; Socrates is a man; therefore Socrates is mortal." How do you know that all men are mortal? You know it by induction, and like everything known by induction, you only know it as highly probable, not as certain. "All men are mortal" is itself the conclusion of an argument, in which the premises are: A died, B died, C died, and so on. Since all the people now living have not died, you will have to frame your premises so that the existing population shall not be an argument against your conclusion. Assuming that there is no recorded case of a man living as much as 150 years, you can take as your premise: "A, B, C, . . . have not lived 150 years." To this there are no known exceptions. You may go on to argue: "Therefore probably all men die before they are

150 years old," and then you may make your deduction as to Socrates (whom we are supposing still alive). But this is a foolish detour. Your premises, if they make the general statement probable, make the statement about Socrates considerably more probable; for if there were a few very rare exceptions, it is unlikely that Socrates would happen to be one of them, but your general statement would be false. It is better to say: "In all recorded instances, men have died before reaching the age of 150; therefore probably the same thing will happen in this instance."

This, however, is an argument by simple enumeration, and, as we saw, such arguments can be strengthened by the discovery of general laws, which make our particular case an instance of a much wider generalization. Instead of confining ourselves to men, we can take account of all multicellular animals and plants. We may be able to go farther, and consider the causes which lead chemical compounds to change their chemical composition. That is why the search for general laws is so important. They give increased certainty, not by substituting deduction for induction, but by giving a wider basis to the fundamental enumerations upon which all inductions depend.

The most important use of deduction is in inferring the consequences of hypotheses which are to be tested by observation or experiment. If a hypothesis is true, all its deductive consequences are true; if it is false, some of its consequences are still true, but some are false. Therefore if all the consequences that we can test turn out to be true, it seems probable that the hypothesis is true or nearly true. The drawing of consequences often involves very difficult mathematics, and that is the reason for the importance of mathematics in discovering general laws. When the laws are accepted as established, mathematics is important in drawing consequences which are now accepted as true. Often it is essential to have reason to accept the consequences in advance of experiment. For example, if a railway bridge is to be built, we do not wish to have to wait till a train goes over it before knowing that it is stable. In such a case we rely confidently upon the general laws inferred by induction from previous experiments. There is *some* chance the induction is mistaken, but it is much less than the other hazards to which practical life is exposed—for example, fraud on the part of the contractor who is to build the bridge.

From the time of Pythagoras until the rise of modern science in the 17th Century the example of mathematics misled the learned as to the way in which we acquire knowledge, and as to the most useful kind of logic. It was thought that we know general premises by intuition, or by divine illumination, or by reminiscence from a previous existence. If this were indeed the case, everything that we have to infer could be inferred by deduction. This was not quite the view of Aristotle, who left a place for induction; but it was, to all intents and purposes, the view of Thomas Aquinas. It followed, of course, that observation plays a very subordinate part in the acquisition of knowledge. Aristotle had announced, apparently on religious grounds, that everything in the heavens, unless it is below the moon, is indestructible. This made it impossible to arrive at a correct theory of meteors and new stars. Those who made observations showing that the old theory was wrong were thought wicked, and the facts that they reported were ignored. This over-emphasis on deduction, which was bound up with the belief in self-evident general principles, was one of the causes of the scientific sterility of the middle ages. It was, of course, connected with the essentially deductive character of theology, and with the general religious outlook of the times.

The reader will have noticed, in what we have been saying, the frequent mention of probability. This is characteristic of modern logic as contrasted with that of antiquity and the middle ages. The modern logician realizes that all our knowledge is only probable in a greater or less degree, not certain and indubitable as philosophers and theologians used to think. He is not greatly troubled by the fact that inductive inferences only give probability to their conclusions, for he does not expect anything better. But he is troubled if he finds reason to doubt whether induction can even make a conclusion probable.

There are thus two problems which assume much greater importance in modern logic than in that of former times. The first is as to the nature of probability, and the second is as to the validity of induction. I shall say a few words about each in turn.

Probability is of two sorts, which may be called respectively *definite* and *indefinite*. The definite sort is what is dealt with in the mathematical theory of probability; it has to do with such matters as throwing dice and tossing coins. It arises wherever there are a number of possibilities, and we have no reason to expect one rather than another. If you toss a coin, it must come either heads or tails, but one seems just as likely as the other. Therefore the chance of each is a half, 1 being taken to represent certainty. Similarly if you throw a die, there are six faces upon which it may fall, and you have no ground for thinking one more likely than another, so the chance of each is one sixth. The probability used by insurance companies in their business is of this sort. They do not know which building will be burnt, but they know what percentage of buildings burn in an average year. They do not know how long any particular person will live, but they know the average expectation of life at any given age. In all such cases, the estimate of probability is not itself merely probable, except in the sense in which all knowledge is merely probable. The estimate of a probability may itself have a high degree of certainty. If this were not the case, insurance companies would go bankrupt.

Strenuous efforts have been made to bring the probability of an induction under this head, but there is reason to think that all such attempts have been fallacious. The probability conferred by induction seems to be always of the sort that I have called *indefinite*. This sort must now be explained.

It is a truism that all human knowledge is liable to error. The liability to error obviously has degrees. If I say that Buddha lived in the 6th Century B.C., the liability to error is obviously very great. If I say that Caesar was assassinated, the chance of error is less. If I say that a great war is being fought at the present time, there is so slight a possibility of error that only a philosopher or a logician would admit its existence. These examples have to do with historical events, but there is a similar gradation as regards scientific laws. Some are admittedly hypotheses, to which no one would give serious credence in the absence of further evidence, while others seem so certain that no practical important doubt as to their truth is entertained by men of science. (When I say "truth" I mean "approximate truth," for every scientific law is liable to small emendations.) This sort of thing, which distinguishes between what we firmly believe and what we are only more or less inclined to admit, ought not to be called *probability,* if that word is understood as in the mathematical theory of probability. It would be better to speak of *degrees of doubtfulness* or *degrees of credibility.* This is a vaguer conception than what I have called "definite probability," but it is also a more important conception.

Let us take an illustration. If you are on a jury which is engaged in a murder trial, the judge will tell you that you must bring in a verdict of "guilty" if there can be no *reasonable* doubt that the accused committed the crime. If you have studied logic, you may ask the judge what degree of doubt is "reasonable," but unless he has *not* studied logic, he will be unable to give you a definite answer. He cannot say "there is reasonable doubt if the odds in favor of the man's guilt are less than 100 to 1," because there is no means of reckoning the odds. You cannot get a series of exactly similar trials, together with data as to whether the verdict was right or wrong. And yet every jury, with few exceptions, arrives at a verdict, usually with a considerable degree of confidence in its own rightness.

It is this somewhat vague concept that is invoked when it is said that all our knowledge is open to question. The question what degree of doubt is "reasonable" depends upon your purpose. There may be reasonable doubt from the standpoint of a philosopher or a logician when there is none from the standpoint of a juryman. From the point of view of the logician, the important thing is to decide upon the *degree* of credibility of various statements. As to this, there would be a certain measure of agreement. Most people would give the highest place to such statements as "2 and 2 are 4"; to feel them doubtful would be almost pathological. Statements about what we are experiencing at the moment, such as "I am hot" or "I hear a loud noise," if they are carefully interpreted, have a very high place in the order of comparative certainty. Vivid recent memories are less reliable, but become almost certain if they are confirmed by a number of other people. Some things in history and geography are not questioned by any sensible person—for instance, the past existence of Napoleon and the present existence of Mount Everest. It is only slightly less certain that the earth is round and that the planets go round the sun in orbits which are approximately elliptical. In all this, I am speaking, not as a philosopher, but as an interpreter of educated common sense.

Now if, as a logician, you ask yourself what is the nature of your evidence for beliefs which are virtually but not theoretically certain, such as those about Napoleon and Mount Everest, you will find that, in every case, the evidence is only good if the principle of induction, in some form, is admitted. Why do we believe in Napoleon? Because of testimony. Why do we believe in testimony? Because we think it unlikely that a number of people, independently, would all invent the same story. Why? Because experience shows that liars usually disagree unless they are in a conspiracy. Ultimately, we must reach a point where we use experience of what is known as a basis for inferring what is unknown, and this sort of inference is only valid if induction is valid.

Laplace thought that the probability involved in an inductive inference was *definite* probability, and could be measured numerically. He had a principle from which it would follow that, if you came into a Welsh village and asked the first man you met what his name was, and he said "Williams," then the odds were two to one that the next man you met would be called Williams. If he was, the odds for the next man would be three to one, and so on: if the first 100 were all called Williams, the odds for the 101st would be 101 to 1. If this principle were valid, the inductions of science, especially when, by means of laws, many are collected together into one vast induction, would have such enormous odds in their favor that no practical man need bother with the chance of their turning out wrong. Unfortunately, however, Laplace's reasoning involved fallacies, and is now generally rejected. We cannot so easily, if at all, reach a numerical estimate of the probability of inductions.

Hume, who allowed himself to be skeptical about everything, threw doubt on the principle of induction. Since his day, logicians have written much on the problem, but without solving it. Broadly speaking, there are three possibilities. First, the principle may be demonstrable. Second, though not demonstrable, it may be accepted as self-evident. Third, it may be rejected as a mere animal habit incapable of rational justification. To all three of these there are objections.

Attempts to demonstrate the principle, such as that of Laplace, have all broken down. And to any one accustomed to considering what can be deduced from what, it must seem very improbable that a proof could be found, except by assuming some other principle, such as the reign of law, which stands just as much in need of proof. Although we cannot say dogmatically that a proof will never be found, the possibility must be regarded as very slight.

Can we say that the principle is "self-evident"? It is not clear, in the first place, what this would mean. One may say that something is self-evident to you when you cannot help believing it; but in this case what is self-evident may be false. It used to be self-evident that there could not be people at the antipodes, because they would fall off. We may strengthen the definition of "self-evidence"; we may say that something is "self-evident" when no one can doubt it, however hard he may try. If we adopt this definition, we must say that the principle is not self-evident because Hume succeeded in doubting it. There is an odd circumstance about inductive inferences, that the conclusion presents itself to the unreflective mind as indubitable, although the inference, when formally stated, seems open to question. To revert to an earlier instance: Experience of apples causes you to expect confidently that *this* apple, which you are about to eat, will taste like an apple and not like a beefsteak. The inductive logician tries to turn this into an argument: "Since former apples tasted like apples, so will this one." But in fact former apples are probably not in your thoughts. You have an expectation about *this* apple, which has causes in your physiology, but not grounds in your thinking. When the logician tries to find grounds, he also tries to weaken your confidence; he tells you it is only *probable* that this apple will not taste like a beefsteak. At this point you will probably say: "Away with logicians! They only try to confuse me about things that everybody knows perfectly well." But what everybody knows, or thinks he knows, are the *conclusions* of inductions, not their connection with the premises. It is the body rather than the mind that does the connecting of premises and conclusion in an induction. The attempt to treat the inductive principle itself as self-evident seems, therefore, to break down.

Shall we then agree with the skeptic, and say "away with induction! It is a superstition, and I will have none of it"? The skeptic can answer most of the objections that you may feel inclined to bring against him. You may say: "Well, at least you must admit that induction works." "*Has* worked, you mean," the skeptic will reply: for it is only induction itself that assures us that what has worked will work. Perhaps tomorrow stones will be nourishing and bread will be poison, the sun will be cold and the moon hot. The cause of our disbelief in such possibilities is our animal habits; but these equally might change, and we might suddenly begin to expect the opposite of everything that we expect at present.

To this argument Professor Reichenbach, who is a great authority on probability, has offered a kind of answer. Roughly speaking, his answer is this: If induction is valid, science is possible; if it is not, science is impossible, since there is no other imaginable principle to take its place. Therefore you will do well to act on the assumption that induction is valid, since, otherwise, you can have no reason for doing one thing rather than another. This answer is not fallacious, but I cannot say that I find it very satisfying. I hope, and I more or less believe, that in time a better answer will be found. If you, reader, become a logician, it may be you who will find this better answer.

I do not know whether the usefulness of logic has become evident in the course of what has been said, but in case it has not, we may end with a few words on this subject.

We are all perpetually making or accepting inferences, and many of these, though persuasive at first sight, are in fact invalid. When we act on an invalid inference, we are likely to fail in achieving our ends. In politics and economics, most of the argumentation is fallacious. Spain, in the 16th Century, was ruined by accepting an argument professing to show that gold ought to be kept at home. I will not adduce more recent instances, for fear of becoming involved in political controversy. I will, however, say this: At the end of the present war, reconstruction will demand much clear thinking, and wide-spread popular fallacies will be a very great obstacle to desirable measures of statesmanship. Science, which is, at present, more amenable to logic than politics, has achieved great triumphs; if similar triumphs are to be achieved in other departments of social life, it will be necessary that men shall learn to think more logically, and less as the slaves of prejudice and passion. Perhaps such a hope is utopian; perhaps, however, the lessons of experience may weaken the hold of the irrational creeds that infest the modern world.

The Art of Reckoning

*W*E LIVE in a technical civilization, of which most of us understand very little. Why does electric light go on when you press the switch? Why is it cold in the ice-box? How do airmen take aim at a target from a fast-moving aeroplane? What enables astronomers to predict eclipses? On what principles do insurance companies decide what to charge? These are all very practical questions; unless some one knew the answer, we could not enjoy the comforts upon which we are wont to pride ourselves. But those who know the answers are few. Usually these few invent a rule or a machine which enables other people to get on with very little knowledge; a practical electrician does not have to know the theory of electricity, though this was necessary for the inventions which he knows how to manipulate. If you want to be able to answer such every-day questions, you have to learn many things; the most indispensable of these is mathematics.

Some people will always dislike mathematics, however well they may be taught. They ought not to try to become mathematicians, and their teachers ought to let them off after they have proved their inefficiency over the rudiments. But if mathematics were properly taught, there would be very much fewer people who would hate it than there are at present.

There are various ways of stimulating a love of mathematics. One is the method unintentionally adopted by Galileo's father, who was himself a teacher of mathematics, but found himself unable to make a living by his profession. He determined that his son should do something more lucrative, and with that end in view concealed from the youth the very existence of mathematics. But one day—so the story goes—the boy, now 18 years old, happened to overhear a lecture on geometry which was being given by a man in the next room. He was fascinated, and within a very short time became one of the leading mathematicians of the age. However, I doubt if this method is quite suitable for adoption by educational authorities. I think perhaps there are other methods that are likely to be more widely successful.

In the early stages, all teaching of mathematics should start from practical problems; they should be easy problems, and such as might seem interesting to a child. When I was young (perhaps things have not changed in this respect) the problems were such as no one could possibly *wish* to solve. For instance: A, B, and C are travelling from X to Y. A on foot, B on a horse, and C on a bicycle. A is always going to sleep at odd moments, B's horse goes lame, and C has a puncture. A takes twice as long as B would have taken if his horse hadn't gone lame, and C gets there half an hour after A would have got there if he hadn't gone to sleep—and so on. Even the most ardent pupil is put off by this sort of thing.

The best way, in teaching, is to take a hint from the early history of mathematics. The subject was invented because there were practical problems that people really *wished* to solve, either from curiosity or for some urgent practical reason. The Greeks told endless stories about such problems and the clever men who found out how to deal with them. No doubt these stories are often untrue, but that does not matter when they are used as illustrations. I shall repeat a few of them, without vouching for their historical accuracy.

The founder of Greek mathematics and philosophy was Thales, who was a young man in 600 B.C. In the course of his travels he went to Egypt, and the king of Egypt asked him if he could find out the height of the Great Pyramid. Thales, at a given moment, measured the length of its shadow and of his own. It was obvious that the proportion of his height to the length of his shadow was the same as the proportion of the height of the pyramid to the length of its shadow, and so the answer was found by the rule of three. The king then asked him if he could find out the distance of a ship at sea without leaving the land. This is a more difficult problem, and he can hardly have given a general solution, although tradition says that he did. The principle is to observe the direction of the ship from two points on the coast which are at a known distance apart; the further off the ship is, the less difference there will be in the two directions. The complete answer requires trigonometry, which did not exist until many centuries after the time of Thales. But in particular cases the answer is easy. Suppose, for instance, that the coast runs east and west, that the ship is due north of a certain point A on the coast, and due north-west of a certain other point B. Then the distance from A to the ship will be the same as the distance from A to B, as the reader can easily convince himself by drawing a figure. Supposing the ship part of a hostile navy, and Egyptian troops draw up on the shore to oppose it, this knowledge might be very useful.

Serious mathematics began with the proposition known as the theorem of Pythagoras. The Egyptians had made some slight beginnings in geometry, in order—so it is said—to be able to measure out their fields again when the Nile flood subsided. They had noticed that a triangle whose sides are respectively 3, 4, and 5 units of length has a right angle. Pythagoras (or some one belonging to his school) noticed a curious fact about this triangle. If you make squares on the sides of a triangle of this kind, one square will have 9 square units, another 16, and the third 25; now 9 and 16 are 25. Pythagoras (or a disciple) generalized this, and proved that in any right-angled triangle the squares on the shorter sides are together equal to the square on the longest side. This was a most important discovery, and encouraged the Greeks to construct the science of geometry, which they did with amazing skill.

But out of this discovery a worry arose, which troubled both the Greeks and the mathematicians of modern times, and has only been fully solved in our own day. Suppose you have a right-angled triangle in which each of the shorter sides is one inch long; how long will the third side be? The square on each of the shorter sides is one square inch; so the square on the longer side will measure two square inches. So the length of the longer side must be some number of inches such that, when you multiply this number by itself, you get 2. This number is called "the square root of 2." The Greeks soon discovered that there is no such number. You can easily persuade yourself of this. The number can't be a whole number, because 1 is too small and 2 is too big. But if you multiply a fraction by itself, you get another fraction, not a whole number; so there cannot be any fraction which, multiplied by itself, gives 2. So the square root of 2 is neither a whole number nor a fraction. What else it could be remained a mystery, but mathematicians continued hopefully to use it and talk about it, in the expectation that some day they would discover what they meant. In the end this expectation proved justified.

A similar problem arose as to what is called "the cube root of 2," that is to say, a number x such that x times x times x is 2. A certain city—so the story runs—had been dogged by misfortunes, and at last sent to consult the oracle of Apollo at Delphi as to the cause of the series of disasters. The god replied that the statue of himself in his temple in that city was too small, and he wanted one twice as large. The citizens were eager to comply with the divine commands, and at first they thought of making a statue twice as high as the old one. But then they realized that it would be also twice as broad and twice as thick, so that it would need eight times as much material, and would, in fact, be eight times as large. This would be going beyond what the oracle ordained, and would be a waste of money. How much taller, then, must the new statue be, if, altogether, it was to be twice as large? The citizens sent a deputation to Plato, to ask if any one in his academy could give them the answer. He set the mathematicians to work on the problem. But after some centuries they decided that it was insoluble. It could, of course, be solved approximately, but, as in the case of the square root of 2, there is no fraction that solves it exactly. Though the problem was not solved, much useful work was done in the course of looking for a solution.

Leaving the ancients for the present, let us come to the problems of insurance companies. Suppose you wish to insure your life, so that your widow will get $1,000 when you die. How much ought you to pay every year? Let us suppose your age such that the average man of your age will live another 20 years. If you pay $50 a year, you will, in

20 years, have paid $1,000, and at first sight you might think it a fair bargain if the insurance company asked you to pay $50 a year. But in fact this would be too much, because of interest. Assuming you live 20 years, your first $50 will be invested by the insurance company, and will bring interest; the interest will be invested, and so on; so that you have to calculate what your $50 will amount to in 20 years at compound interest. For the next $50, you have to calculate what it will amount to in 19 years at compound interest, and so on. In this way, your payments will have brought the insurance company much more than $1,000 by the end of the 20 years. In fact, if the insurance company gets 4 percent on its investments, your payments of $50 a year will have brought in about $1,500 at the end of the 20 years. To work out sums of this sort, you have to know how to add up what are called "geometrical progressions."

A "geometrical progression" is a series of numbers in which each, after the first, is a fixed multiple of its predecessor. For instance, 1, 2, 4, 8, 16, . . . is a geometrical progression in which each number is double of its predecessor; 1, 3, 9, 27, 81, . . . is a geometrical progression in which each number is three times its predecessor; 1, ½, ¼, ⅛, $^1/_{16}$, . . . is one in which each number is half its predecessor, and so on.

Now let us return to our dollar invested at 4 percent compound interest. At the end of the year, it amounts to $1.04. At the end of the second year, you have $1.04 and a year's interest on it; this is 1.04 times 1.04, i. e. $(1.04)^2$. At the end of the third year, it amounts to $(1.04)^3$, and so on. And so, if you pay a dollar a year for 20 years, at the end of the 20th year what you have paid has become worth

$(1.04)^{20}$ plus $(1.04)^{19}$ plus . . . plus $(1.04)^2$ plus 1.04 which is a geometrical progression.

The ancients took much interest in geometrical progressions, particularly in those that go on forever. For instance, ½ plus ¼ plus ⅛ plus $^1/_{16}$ plus . . . for ever adds up to 1. So does the recurring decimal .9999. . . . This led to all sorts of puzzles, which took a long time to solve.

Ancient geometry concerned itself not only with straight lines and circles, but also with "conic sections," which are the various sorts of curves that can be made by the intersection of a plane and a cone; or again they can be defined as all the possible shapes of the shadow of a circle on a wall. The Greeks studied them simply for pleasure, without any idea of practical utility, which they despised. But after about 2,000 years, in the 17th Century, they were suddenly found to be of the greatest practical importance. The development of artillery had shown people that if you want to hit a distant object, you must not aim straight at it, but a little above it. No one knew exactly how a cannon ball traveled, but military commanders were anxious to know. Galileo, who was employed by the Duke of Tuscany, discovered the answer: they travel in parabolas, which are a particular kind of conic section. At about the same time Kepler discovered that the planets go round the sun in ellipses, which are another kind of conic section. In this way all the work that had been done on conic sections became useful in warfare, navigation, and astronomy.

I spoke a moment ago of conic sections as shadows of circles. You can make the different kinds of conic sections for yourself if you have a lamp with a circular lampshade. The shadow of the lampshade on the ceiling (unless it is crooked) will be another circle, but the shadow on the wall will be a hyperbola. If you take a piece of paper and hold it above the lampshade, if you hold it not quite horizontal the shadow will be an ellipse; as you slope it more, the ellipse will get longer and thinner; the first shadow that is not an ellipse, as you slope the piece of paper more and more, is a parabola; after that, it becomes a hyperbola. Falling drops in a fountain make a parabola; so do stones thrown over a cliff.

Mathematically, as any one can see, the subject of shadows is the same as perspective. The study of the properties which a figure has in common with all its possible shadows is called "projective" geometry; although it is really simpler than the sort of geometry that the Greeks did, it was discovered much later. One of the pioneers in this subject was Pascal, who, unfortunately, decided that religious meditation was more important than mathematics.

I have not hitherto said anything about

algebra, which owed its beginning to the very late Alexandrian Greeks, but was mainly developed, first by the Arabs, and then by the men of the 16th and 17th Centuries. Algebra, at first, is apt to seem more difficult than geometry, because in geometry there is a concrete figure to look at, whereas the x's and y's of algebra are wholly abstract. Algebra is only generalized arithmetic: when there is some proposition which is true of *any* number, it is a waste of time to prove it for each separate number, so we say "let x be any number" and proceed with our reasoning. Suppose, for instance, you notice that 1 plus 3 is 4, which is twice 2; 1 plus 3 plus 5 is 9, which is 3 times 3; 1 plus 3 plus 5 plus 7 is 16, which is 4 times 4. It may occur to you to wonder whether this is a general rule, but you will need algebra to express at all simply the question you are asking yourself, which is: "Is the sum of the first n odd numbers always n^2?" When you have come to the point of being able to understand this question, you will easily find a proof that the answer is *yes*. If you don't use a letter such as n, you have to use very complicated language. You can say: "If any number of odd numbers, starting from 1 and missing none, are added up, the result is the square of the number of odd numbers added." This is much more difficult to understand. And when we reach more complicated questions, it soon becomes quite impossible to understand them without the use of letters instead of the phrase "any number."

Even problems that have to do with particular numbers are often much easier to solve if we use the letter x for the number we want. When I was very young I was puzzled by the conundrum: "If a fish weighs 5 lbs, and half its own weight, how much does it weigh?" Many people are inclined to say 7½ lbs. If you begin "let x be the weight of the fish," and go on "5 lbs added to one-half of x equals x," it is obvious that 5 lbs is half of x, so that x is 10 lbs. This problem is almost too easy to need "x." Take one just a little more difficult. The police are pursuing a criminal along a certain road; he has 10 minutes start, but the police car can do 70 miles an hour, while the criminal's car can only do 60. How long will it take them to catch up with him? The answer of course is 1 hour. This can be "seen" in one's head; but if I said the criminal had 7 minutes start, his car could do 53 miles an hour, and the police car could do 67, you would find it best to begin: Let t be the number of minutes it will take the police to catch up. Getting used to the algebraic use of letters is difficult for a boy or girl beginning algebra. It should be made easy by first giving a great many instances of a general formula. For instance:

11 times 11 is 10 times 10 plus twice 10 plus 1

12 times 12 is 11 times 11 plus twice 11 plus 1

13 times 13 is 12 times 12 plus twice 12 plus 1, and so on,

and in the end it becomes easy to understand that

n plus 1 times n plus 1 is n times n plus twice n plus 1.

In the early stages of teaching algebra, this process should be repeated with each new formula.

One of the odd things about mathematics is that, in spite of its great practical utility, it seems, in much of the detail, like a mere frivolous game. No one is likely to become good at mathematics unless he enjoys the game for its own sake. Skilled work, of no matter what kind, is only done well by those who take a certain pleasure in it, quite apart from its utility, either to themselves in earning a living, or to the world through its outcome. No one can become a good mathematician *merely* in order to earn a living, or *merely* in order to be a useful citizen; he must also get the kind of satisfaction from mathematics that people get from solving bridge problems or chess problems. I will therefore give a few examples. If they amuse you, it may be worth your while to devote a good deal of time to mathematics; if not, not.

I remember that, as a boy, I discovered for myself, with great delight, the formula for the sum of what is called an "arithmetical progression." An arithmetical progression is a series of numbers in which each term after the first is greater (or less) than its predecessor by a fixed amount. This fixed amount is called the "common difference." The series 1, 3, 5, 7, . . . is an arithmetical progression, in which the common difference is 2. The series 2, 5, 8, 11, . . . is an arithmetical progression in which the common difference is 3. Suppose now you have an arithmetical progression consisting of a finite number of terms, and you want to know what all the terms together add up to. How will you proceed?

Let us take an easy example: the series 4, 8, 12, 16, . . . up to 96, that is to say, all numbers less than 100 that divide by 4. If you want to know what all these add up to, you can of course do the sum straight forwardly. But you can save yourself this trouble by a little observation. The first term is 4, the last is 96; these add up to 100. The second term is 8, the last but one is 92; these again add up to 100. So it is obvious that you can take the numbers in pairs, and that each pair will add up to 100. There are 24 numbers, therefore there are 12 pairs, therefore the sum you want is 1200. This suggests the general rule: To find the sum of an arithmetical progression, add together the first and last terms, and then multiply by half the numbers of terms. You can easily persuade yourself that this is right, not only when the number of terms is even, as in the above example, but also when it is odd.

But we may want to get a new form for

this formula, if we have not been told what the last term is, but only the first term, the number of terms, and the common difference. Let us take an example. Suppose the first term is 5, the common difference is 3, and the number of terms is 21. Then the last term will be 5 plus 20 times 3, i.e. 65. So the sum of the first and last terms is 70, and the sum of the series is half of this multiplied by the number of terms, i.e. half of 70 times 21. This is 35 times 21, i.e. 735. The rule is: Add twice the first term to the common difference multiplied by one less than the number of terms in the series, and then multiply all this by half the number of terms in the series. This is the same as the earlier rule, but differently expressed.

Now let us take another problem. Suppose you had a number of tanks, each a perfect cube, i.e. having length, breadth, and depth all equal. Suppose the first is 1 foot each way, the second 2, the third 3, and so on. You wish to know how many cubic feet of oil you can get them all to hold. The first will hold 1 cubic foot, the second 8, the third 27, the fourth 64, the fifth 125, the sixth 216, and so on. So what you want to find is the sum of the cubes of the first so many numbers. You notice that

1 & 8 make 9, i.e. 3 times 3, and 3 is half of 2 times 3.

1 & 8 & 27 make 36, i.e. 6 times 6, and 6 is half of 3 times 4.

1 & 8 & 27 & 64 make 100, i.e. 10 times 10, and 10 is half of 4 times 5.

1 & 8 & 27 & 64 & 125 make 225, i.e. 15 times 15, and 15 is half of 5 times 6.

1 & 8 & 27 & 64 & 125 & 216 make 441,

i.e. 21 times 21, and 21 is half of 6 times 7. This suggests a rule for the sum of the cubes of the first so many whole numbers. The rule is: Multiply the number of whole numbers concerned by one more than itself, take half of this product, and then take the square of the number you have now got. You can easily persuade yourself that this formula is always right, by what is called "mathematical induction." This means: assume your formula is right up to a certain number, and prove that in that case it is right for the next number. Notice that your formula is right for 1. Then it follows that it is right for 2, and therefore for 3, and so on. This is a very powerful method, by which a great many of the properties of whole numbers are proved. It often enables you, as in the above case, to turn a guess into a theorem.

Let us consider another kind of problem, which is called that of "combinations and permutations." This kind of problem is often of great importance, but we will begin with trivial examples. Suppose a hostess wishes to give a dinner party, and there are 20 people to whom she owes an invitation, but she can only ask 10 at a time. How many possible ways are there of making a selection? Obviously there are 20 ways of choosing the first guest; when he has been chosen, there are 19 ways of choosing the next; and so on. When 9 guests have been chosen, there are 11 possibilities left, so the last guest can be chosen in 11 ways. So the whole number of possible choices is

20 times 19 times 18 times 17 times 16 times 15 times 14 times 13 times 12 times 11.

This is quite a large number; it is a miracle that hostesses do not become more bewildered. We can simplify the statement of the answer by using what are called "factorials."

Factorial 2 means the product of all the

numbers up to 2, i.e. 2

Factorial 3 means the product of all the numbers up to 3, i.e. 6

Factorial 4 means the product of all the numbers up to 4, i.e. 24

Factorial 5 means the product of all the numbers up to 5, i.e. 120

and so on. Now the number of possible choices we had above is factorial 20 divided by factorial 10. This is a problem in what is called "combinations." The general rule is that the number of ways in which you can choose m things out of n things (n being greater than m) is factorial n divided by factorial m.

Now let us consider "permutations," where the question is not what things to choose, but how to arrange them. Our hostess, we will suppose, has chosen her 10 guests, and is now considering how to seat them. She and her husband have fixed places, at the head and foot of the table, and the guests have to be distributed among the 10 other places. So there are 10 possibilities for the first guest, and when his place is fixed there are 9 for the next, and so on; thus the total number of possibilities is factorial

10, i.e. 3,628,800. Fortunately, social rules, such as alternating men and women and separating husbands and wives, reduce the effective possibilities to 4 or 5.

Let us take one more problem in "combinations." Suppose you have a number of objects, and you may choose as many or as few of them as you like, and may even choose all or none. How many choices have you?

If there is one object A, you have 2 choices, A or none.

If there are 2, A and B, you have 4 choices, A and B, or A, or B, or none.

If there are 3, A and B and C, you have 8 choices, A and B and C, A and B, A and C, B and C, A, B, C, or none.

If there are 4, you have 16, and so on. The general rule is that the number of choices is 2 multiplied by itself as many times as there are objects. This is really obvious, because you have two possibilities in regard to each object, namely to choose it or reject it, and when you have made your choice in regard to one object you still have complete freedom as regards the others.

Problems of permutations and combinations have an enormous number of applications. One of them is in the Mendelian theory of heredity. The first biologists who revived Mendel's work knew almost no mathematics, but they found certain numbers constantly turning up. One of them mentioned this to a mathematical friend, who at once pointed out that they are numbers which occur in the theory of combinations, and when this had been noticed the reason was easy to see. Nowadays Mendelism is full of mathematics: take, for instance, such a problem as this: if a certain recessive characteristic gives you an advantage in the struggle for existence, will it tend to become general in a population in which it sometimes occurs? And, if so, how long will it take to belong to some given percentage of the population, if we know the percentage having this characteristic at present? Such problems are often of great practical importance, for instance, in regard to the spread of feeble-mindedness and other mental defects.

The great merit of modern as compared with ancient mathematics is that it can deal with continuous change. The only kind of motion that could be dealt with by ancient or medieval mathematics was uniform motion in a straight line or a circle: Aristotle had said that it was "natural" for earthly bodies to move in straight lines and heavenly bodies in circles, a view which persisted until Kepler and Galileo showed that it had no application to the facts. The technical instrument for dealing with continuous change is the differential and integral calculus, invented independently by Newton and Leibniz.

We may illustrate the use of the calculus by considering what is meant by "velocity." Suppose you are in a train which has lately started from a station and is still gaining speed, and you want to know how fast it is moving at the present moment. We will suppose that you know how far apart the telegraph poles are, so that you can estimate the distance the train has traversed in a given time. You find, let us suppose, that in the second after the moment at which you wished to know the speed of the train it has traversed 44 feet. 44 feet a second is 30 miles an hour, so you say "we were doing 30 miles an hour." But although this was your average speed throughout the second, it was not your speed at the beginning, because the train is accelerating, and was moving faster towards the end of the second than at the beginning. If you were able to measure sufficiently accurately, you might find that in the first quarter of a second the train traveled 10 feet, not 11. So the speed of the train at the beginning of the second was nearer 40 feet than 44. But 40 feet per second will still be too much, since even in a quarter of a second there will have been *some* acceleration. If you can measure small times and distances accurately, the shorter the time you take for estimating the train's speed the more nearly right you will be. But you will never be *quite* right.

What, then, can be meant by the speed of the train at a given instant? This is the question that is answered by the differential calculus. You make a series of closer and closer approximations to its speed by taking shorter and shorter times. If you take one second, your estimate is 44 feet per second; if you take a quarter of a second, it is 40. We will suppose that there are men on the edge of the railway with stopwatches; they find that if you take a tenth of a second, the speed works out at 39.2 feet per second; if a twentieth of a second, at 39.1, and so on. Imagining an impossible accuracy of measurement and observation, we may suppose that the observers find, as they make the times shorter and shorter, that the speed as estimated is always slightly above 39, but is not always above any number greater than 39. Then 39 is called the "limit" of the series of numbers, and we say that 39 feet per second is the velocity of the train at the given instant. This is the *definition* of velocity at an instant.

The "differential calculus" is the mathematical instrument by which, if you know the position of a body at each instant, you calculate its speed at each instant. The "integral calculus" deals with the opposite problem: given the direction and speed of motion of a body at each instant, to calculate where it will be each instant, given the place from which it started. The two together are called the "calculus."

A simple example of a problem that needs the integral calculus is what is called the "curve of pursuit." A farmer and his dog are in a square field, of which the corners are A, B, C, D. At first the dog is at A and the farmer is at B. The farmer begins to walk towards C, and at the same moment whistles to his dog, who runs at a uniform speed always towards where his master is at that moment. What curve will the dog describe.

More important examples are derived from the motions of the planets. Kepler proved by observation that they move round the sun in ellipses, and he discovered a relation between the distances of different planets from the sun and the times it takes them to go round the sun. This enabled Newton, by the differential calculus, to infer the velocity of a planet at any point of its orbit; the velocity is not constant, but greatest when the planet is nearest to the sun. Then, using the differential calculus once more, he could calculate the planet's acceleration at each instant—i.e. its change of velocity both in magnitude and direction. He found that every planet at every moment has an acceleration towards the sun which is inversely proportional to the square of its distance from the sun.

He then took up the inverse problem,

which is one for the integral calculus. If a body has, at every moment, an acceleration towards the sun which is inversely proportional to the square of its distance from the sun, how will it move? He proved that it will move in a conic section. Observation shows that, in the case of the planets and certain comets, this conic section is an ellipse; in the case of certain other comets, it may be a hyperbola. With this his proof of the law of gravitation was complete.

It must not be supposed that the calculus applies only to change in time. It applies wherever one quantity is a continuous "function" of another. The notion of "function" is an important one, which I shall try to explain.

Given a variable quantity, another is said to be a "function" of it if, when the variable quantity is given, the value of the other is determinate. For instance, if you have to transport a quantity of oil by train, the number of tank-cars you will need is a "function" of the quantity of oil; if you have to feed an army, the quantiy of food required is a "function" of the number of soldiers. If a body is falling in a vacuum, the distance it has fallen is a "function" of the time during which it has been falling. The number of square feet of carpet required in a square room is a "function" of the length of the sides, and so is the amount of liquid that can be put into a cubic container; in one case the function is the square, in the other the cube —a room whose sides are twice as long as those of another room will need four times as much carpet, and a cask which is twice as high as another will hold eight times as much liquid, if its other dimensions are increased in proportion.

Some functions are very complicated. Your income tax is a function of your income, but only a few experts know what function. Suppose some mathematically minded expert were to propose a simple function, for instance, that your income tax should be proportional to the square of your income. He might combine this with the proposal that no one's income, after deduction of the tax, should exceed $25,000. How would this work out? The tax would have to be one hundred-thousandth part of the square of your income in dollars. On incomes of less than the square root of $1,000 (which is about $32), the tax would be less than a cent, and would not be collected; on $1,000 the tax would be $10; on $2,000, $40; on $10,000, $1,000 and on $50,000 it would be $25,000. After that, any increase of income would make you poorer. If you had an income of $100,000, the tax would be exactly equal to your income, and you would be penniless. I do not think it very likely that any one will advocate this plan.

Given any function of a variable x, a slight increase in x will be accompanied by a slight increase or decrease of the function unless the function is discontinuous. For instance, let x be the radius of a circle, and let the function concerned be the area of the circle, which is proportional to the square of the radius. If the radius is slightly increased, the area of the circle is increased; the increase is obtained by multiplying the increase of the radius by the circumference. The differential calculus gives the rate of the increase of the function for a given small increase of the variable. On the other hand, if you know the rate of increase of the function relative to the variable, the integral calculus tells you what the total increase or decrease of the function will be as the variable passes from one value to another. The simplest of important instances is that of a body falling in a vacuum. Here the acceleration is constant, that is to say, the increase of velocity in any given time is proportional to the time. Therefore the total velocity at any time is proportional to the length of time since the fall began. From this the integral calculus shows that the total distance fallen since the fall began is proportional to the square of the time since the fall began. This can be proved without the integral calculus, and was so proved by Galileo; but in more complicated cases the calculus is essential.

Mathematics is, at least professedly, an *exact* instrument, and when it is applied to the actual world there is always an unjustified assumption of exactness. There are no exact circles or triangles in nature; the planets do not revolve exactly in ellipses, and if they did we could never know it. Our powers of measurement and observation are limited. I do not mean that they have a *definite* limit; on the contrary, improvement in technique is continually lowering the limit. But it is impossible that any technique should leave no margin of probable error, because, whatever apparatus we may invent, we depend, in the end, upon our senses, which cannot distinguish between two things that are very closely similar. It is easy to prove that there are differences which we cannot perceive. Suppose, for instance, there are three closely similar shades of color, A, B, and C. It may happen that you cannot see any difference between A and B, or between B and C, but you can see a difference between A and C. This shows that there must be imperceptible differences between A and B and between B and C. The same would be true if A, B, C were three nearly equal lengths. The measurement of lengths, however it may be improved, must always remain only approximate, though the approximation may be very close.

For this reason, careful scientific measurements are always given with a "probable error." This means that the result given is as likely as not to be out by the amount of the assigned probable error. It is practically certain to be more or less, but very unlikely to be out *much* more than the probable error.

I wish men in other fields would admit that their opinions were subject to error; but in fact people are most dogmatic where there is least reason for certainty.

The reader who recalls our definition of "velocity" will see that it assumes an impossible minuteness of observation. Empirically, there can be no such thing as the velocity *at an instant,* because there is a lower limit to the times and distances that we can measure. Suppose we could carry our technique so far that we could measure a hundred-thousandth of a second and a hundred-thousandth of a centimeter. We could then tell how far a very small body had moved in a hundred-thousandth of a centimeter, unless it was moving less than a centimeter a second. But we could not tell what it had been doing during that very short time; it might have been traveling uniformly, it might have been going slower at first and then faster, or vice versa, and it might have done the whole distance in one sudden jump. This last hypothesis, which seems bizarre, is actually suggested by quantum theory as the best explanation of certain phenomena. We are in the habit of taking it for granted that space and time and motion are continuous, but we cannot *know* this, because very minute discontinuities would be imperceptible. Until lately, the hypothesis of continuity worked; now it begins to be doubtful whether it has this merit where very minute phenomena are concerned.

The exactness of mathematics is an abstract logical exactness which is lost as soon as mathematical reasoning is applied to the actual world. Plato thought—and many followed him in this—that, since mathematics is in some sense true, there must be an ideal world, a sort of mathematician's paradise, where everything happens as it does in the text-books of geometry. The philosopher, when he gets to heaven (where only philosophers go, according to Plato), will be regaled by the sight of everything that he has missed on earth—perfectly straight lines, exact circles, completely regular dodecahedra, and whatever else is necessary to perfect his bliss. He will then realize that mathematics, though not applicable to the mundane scene, is a vision, at once reminiscent and prophetic, of the better world from which the wise have come and to which they will return. Harps and crowns had less interest for the Athenian aristocrat than for the humble folk who made up the Christian mythology; nevertheless Christian theologians, as opposed to the general run of Christians, accepted much of Plato's account of heaven. When, in modern times, this sort of thing became incredible, an exactness was attributed to Nature, and men of science felt no doubt that the universe works precisely in Newtonian fashion. For Newton's world was one that God could have made; a sloppy, inaccurate, more-or-less-so kind of world, it was felt, would be unworthy of Him. Only in quite recent times has the problem of mathematical exactness, as confronted with the approximate character of sensible knowledge, come to be stated in ways wholly free from all taint of inherited theology.

The result of recent investigations of this problem is to bring in approximateness and inexactitude everywhere, even into the most traditionally sacred regions of logic and arithmetic. To the older logicians, matters were simplified by their belief in immutable natural species. There were cats and dogs, horses and cows; two of each kind had been created by God, two of each kind had gone into the ark, two of a kind, breeding together, always produced offspring of the same kind. And as for Man, was he not distinguished from the brutes by his possession of reason, an immortal soul, and a sense of right and wrong? And so the meanings of such words as "dog," "horse," "man" were perfectly definite, and any living thing to which one of these words was applicable was separated by a finite gulf from all the living things of other kinds. To the question "is this a horse?" there was always an unequivocal and indubitable answer. But to the believer in evolution all this is changed. He holds that the horse evolved gradually out of animals that were certainly not horses, and that somewhere on the way there were creatures that were not definitely horses and not definitely not horses. The same is true of man. Rationality, so far as it exists, has been gradually acquired. Of geological specimens it is impossible to judge whether they had immortal souls or a moral sense, even granting that *we* have these advantages. Various bones have been found which clearly belonged to more or less human bipeds, but whether these bipeds should be called "men" is a purely arbitrary question.

It thus appears that we do not really know what we mean by ordinary every-day words such as "cat" and "dog," "horse" and "man." There is the same sort of uncertainty about the most accurate terms of science, such as "meter" and "second." The meter is defined as the distance between two marks on a certain rod in Paris, when the rod is at a certain temperature. But the marks are not points, and temperature cannot be measured with complete accuracy. Therefore we cannot know *exactly* how long the meter is. Concerning most lengths, we can be sure that they are longer than a meter, or sure that they are shorter. But there remain some lengths of which we cannot be sure whether they are longer or shorter than a meter, or exactly a meter long. The second is defined as the time of swing of a pendulum of a certain length, or as a certain fraction of the day. But we cannot measure accurately either the length of the pendulum or the length of the day. Thus there is just the same trouble about meters and seconds as about horses and dogs, namely that we do not know exactly what the words mean.

"But," you may say, "none of this shakes my belief that 2 and 2 are 4." You are quite right, except in marginal cases—and it is only in marginal cases that you are doubtful whether a certain animal is a dog or a certain length is less than a meter. Two must be two of something, and the proposition "2 and 2 are 4" is useless unless it can be applied. Two dogs and two dogs are certainly four dogs, but cases may arise in which you are doubtful whether two of them are dogs. "Well, at any rate there are four animals," you may say. But there are microorganisms concerning which it is doubtful whether they are animals or plants. "Well then, living organisms," you say. But there are things of which it is doubtful whether they are living organisms or not. You will be driven into saying: "Two entities and two entities are four entities." When you have told me what you mean by "entity," we will resume the argument.

Thus concepts, in general, have a certain region to which they are certainly applicable, and another to which they are certainly inapplicable, but concepts which aim at exactness, like "meter" and "second," though they have a large region (within the approximate field) to which they are certainly inapplicable, have no region at all to which they are certainly applicable. If they are to be made certainly applicable, it must be by sacrificing the claim to exactness.

The outcome of this discussion is that mathematics does not have that exactness to which it apparently lays claim, but is approximate like everything else. This, however, is of no *practical* importance, since in any case all our knowledge of the sensible world is only approximate.

I have gone into this question because, to many people mathematics seems to make a claim to a sort of knowledge superior in kind to that of every day, and this claim, in those who are persuaded that it is not legitimate, rouses a resistance which interferes with their capacity to assimilate mathematical reasoning. The superior certainty of mathematics is only a matter of degree and is due, in so far as it exists, to the fact that mathematical knowledge is really verbal, although this is concealed by its complicated character.

What I have said about exactness so far is not quite the whole of the truth on this question. We cannot know the world exactly, it is true, but we do know that, if we suppose it to be as the mathematicians say, the results are correct as far as we can judge. That is to say, mathematics offers the best working hypotheses for understanding the world. Whenever the current hypotheses seem more or less wrong, it is new mathematics that supply the necessary corrections. Newton's law of gravitation held the field for two and a half centuries, and was then amended by Einstein; but Einstein's universe was quite as mathematical as Newton's. Quantum theory has developed a physics of the atom which is very different from classical physics, but it still works with mathematical symbols and equations. The apparatus of conceptions and operations invented by the pure mathematicians is indispensable in explaining the multiform occurrences in the world as due to the operation of general laws; the only hypotheses that have a chance of being true, in the more advanced sciences, are such as would not occur to any one but a mathematician.

If you wish, therefore, to understand the world theoretically, so far as it can be understood, you must learn a very considerable amount of mathematics. If your interests are practical, and you only wish to manipulate the world, whether for your own profit or for that of mankind, you can, without learning much mathematics, achieve a great deal by building on the work of your predecessors. But a society which confined itself to such work would be, in a sense, parasitic on what had been already discovered. This may be illustrated from the history of radio. Nearly 100 years ago Faraday made a great many ingenious experiments on electromagnetism, but being no mathematician he could not invent really comprehensive hypotheses to explain his results. Then came Clark Maxwell who was not an experimenter but a first-rate mathematician. He inferred from Faraday's experiments that there ought to be electromagnetic waves, and that light must be composed of such electromagnetic waves as had frequencies to which eyes are sensitive. In him this was pure theory. His work belongs to the 70's of the last century. About 20 years after his time or rather less, a German physicist named Hertz, who was both a mathematician and an experimenter, decided to test Maxwell's theory practically, and invented an apparatus by which he could manufacture electromagnetic waves. It turned out that they traveled with the velocity of light, and had all the properties that Maxwell had said they ought to have. Last came Marconi, who made Hertz's invention such as could be used outside the laboratory, for it is Hertz's waves that are used in the radio. This whole development illustrates admirably the interaction of experiment and theory upon which progress in science depends.

Finally, mathematics affords, to those who can appreciate it, very great pleasures to which no moralist can object. In the actual manipulation of the symbols there is the same kind of enjoyment that people find in chess, but it is dignified by being useful and not merely a game. In the sense of understanding something of natural processes there is a feeling of the power of human thought, and in the work of the best mathematicians there is a kind of clear-cut beauty which shows what men can achieve when they free themselves from cowardice and ferocity and from enslavement to the accidents of their corporal existence.